Plants

Plant ABC

Patricia Whitehouse

www.raintreepublishers.co.uk
Visit our website to find out more information about **Raintree** books.

To order:
 Phone 44 (0) 1865 888112
 Send a fax to 44 (0) 1865 314091
 Visit the Raintree Bookshop at **www.raintreepublishers.co.uk** to browse our catalogue and order online.

First published in Great Britain by Raintree, Halley Court, Jordan Hill, Oxford OX2 8EJ, part of Harcourt Education.
Raintree is a registered trademark of Harcourt Education Ltd.

Editorial: Nick Hunter and Diyan Leake
Design: Sue Emerson (HL-US) and Joanna Sapwell (www.tipani.co.uk)
Picture Research: Amor Montes de Oca (HL-US)
Production: Jonathan Smith

Originated by Dot Gradations
Printed and bound in China by South China Printing Company

ISBN 1 844 21068 5
07 06 05 04 03
10 9 8 7 6 5 4 3 2 1

British Library Cataloguing in Publication Data
Whitehouse, Patricia
Plant ABC
575
A full catalogue record for this book is available from the British Library.

Acknowledgements
The publishers would like to thank the following for permission to reproduce photographs: Amor Montes de Oca p. **11**; Color Pic, Inc. pp. **3L** (E. R. Degginger), **22L** (James M. Mejuto), **22R** (Phil Degginger); Craig Mitchelldyer p. **5**; Dick James p. **8**; Dwight Kuhn pp. **4**, **16**, **17**, **23** (root, stem); Eda Rogers p. **9**; Fraser Photos pp. **22** (Greg Beck), **23** (Greg Beck); Holt Photograph Library p. **15**; Jeffrey Rich Nature Photography p. **18**; Marv Binegar p. **19**; Oxford Scientific Films pp. **10**, **21**; Rick Wetherbee p. **3R**; Sally Beyer p. **15** (Greg Ryan); Visuals Unlimited pp. **6** (Tom Edwards), **7** (Mark E. Gibson), **12R** (Jerome Wexler), **13** (Science Vu), **14** (Carol and Dan Spencer), **20** (Inga Spence), **23** (flower, Mark E. Gibson; fruit, Tom Edwards; vein, Inga Spence), back cover (avocado, Inga Spence; ice cream, Jerome Wexler); Winston Fraser pp. **12L**.

Cover photograph of sunflower seeds reproduced with permission of Corbis (Frank Lane Picture Agency)

Every effort has been made to contact copyright holders of any material reproduced in this book. Any omissions will be rectified in subsequent printings if notice is given to the publishers.

Some words are shown in bold, **like this.** You can find them in the glossary on page 23.

Aa apple
Bb blackberry

Apples have seeds inside.

Blackberries have seeds inside, too.

Cc carrot

The orange part of a carrot is its **root**.

Dd dig
Ee eat

People dig carrots out of the ground.

Then we can eat them.

Ff fruit

Seeds grow inside the **fruit**.

Gg garden

A garden is a place to
grow flowers.

Hh hyacinth
Ii iris

hyacinth

iris

Some people grow hyacinths and irises in their gardens.

Jj jasmine

Jasmine flowers smell sweet.

Kk kiwi fruit

Kiwi fruit have lots of **seeds**.

Ll lettuce

Lettuce leaves are good in a salad.

Mm mango
Nn nectarine

Mangoes and nectarines are **fruits** that have a **seed** called a stone inside them.

Oo orange

Oranges have lots of seeds inside.

Pp palm

A palm tree is a kind of plant.

Qq quince

Quinces are hard **fruit** that people make into jam.

Rr root

Roots grow under the ground.

Ss stem

Stems grow above the ground.

Tt tree trunk

This tree trunk is very big.

Uu up

You have to look up to see the top of this tree.

Vv vein

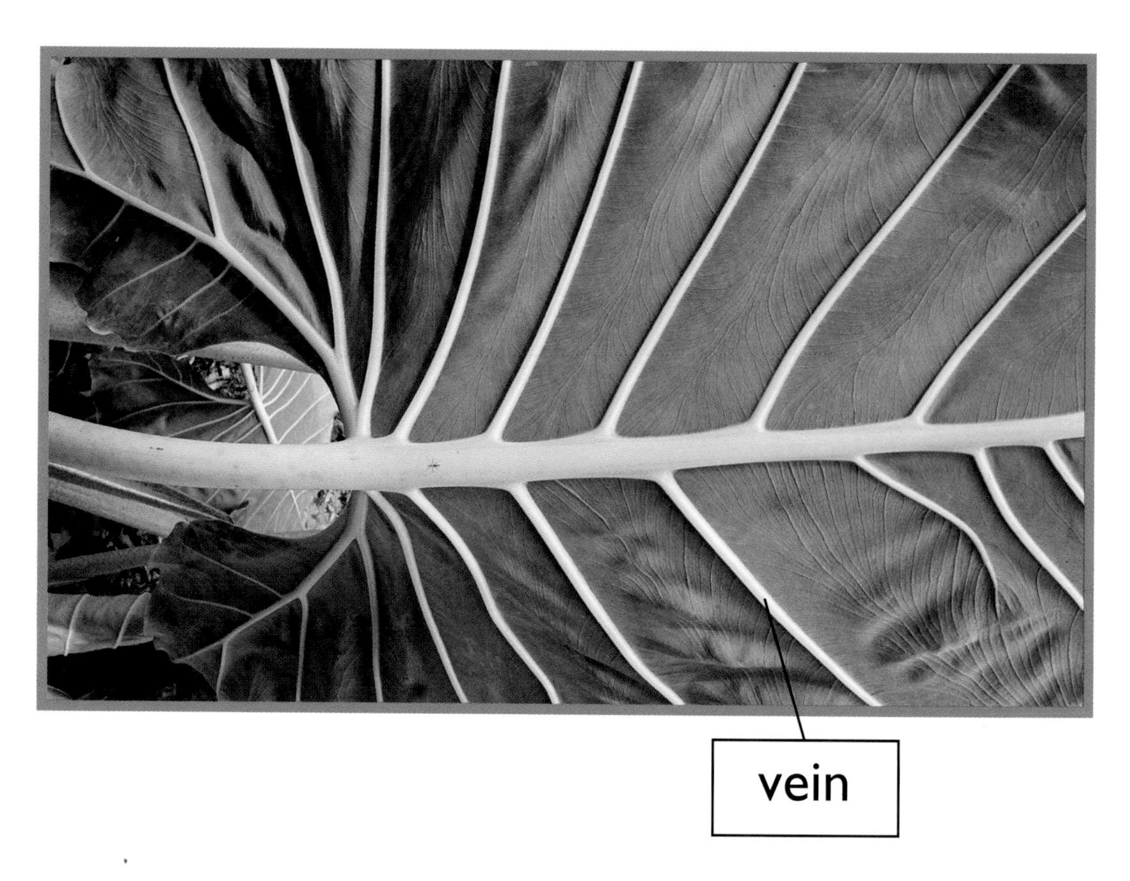

You can see the **veins** in this **leaf**.

Ww   water
Xx   flax

All plants need water.

People grow flax to make a cloth called linen.

Yy yucca
Zz zest

yucca

lemon zest

Yucca plants have pointy leaves.

Lemon **zest** is used to make lemonade.

Glossary

fruit
the part of a plant where the seeds are

leaf
the plant part that is on the stem. It makes food for plants and helps them breathe.

root
the part of a plant that is underground

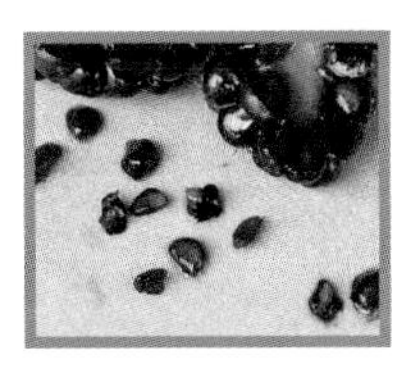

seed
the part that new plants come from

stem
part of a plant where the flowers and leaves grow

vein
thin line on a leaf. Water moves through it.

zest
the skin of a lemon

Index

Titles in the Plants series include:

Hardback 1 844 21064 2

Hardback 1 844 21065 0

Hardback 1 844 21066 9

Hardback 1 844 21067 7

Hardback 1 844 21068 5

Hardback 1 844 21069 3

Find out about the other titles in this series on our website www.raintreepublishers.co.uk